Welcome!

All of the ingredients in this book are safe to use,
but make sure you always follow these rules...

Before You Start

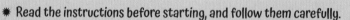

* Read the instructions before starting, and follow them carefully.
* Gather all the ingredients and equipment before you start.
* Don't use any ingredients not listed in the recipes and make sure an adult has checked them over before you start sliming.
* Any slime making should be done under adult supervision. We've highlighted times when a grown up should do something for you.
* No snacking around the slime-making area and when we say slimes cannot be eaten – we mean it! Only ever eat the edible slimes. If you're not sure if you can eat it - check the warning box.
* Keep children under 3 years old and all animals away from your slime experiments.
* Wear eye protection and keep slimy hands away from your eyes.
* Only make and play with slime on hard surfaces – keep away from furniture, carpets, and other items that are hard to clean.
* Watch out when using paint or food colouring – it can stain. Wear rubber gloves so you don't stain your hands.
* Always wash your hands before and after making and playing with slime.
* Clean up after yourself! Wash all equipment and surfaces (see p64).
* A lot of the slimes use eyewash solution. Make sure you use this and not lens cleaner or contact lens solution.
* Don't handle poster paint for too long and wash your hands immediately after using them.

the
Slime
book

Editors Elizabeth Yeates and Clare Lloyd
Jacket design Elle Ward
Pre-production producer
Dragana Puvacic
Senior producer Isabell Schart
Creative director Helen Senior
Cover photography Simon Pask
Photography Tim Pestridge
Publisher Sarah Larter

**Written, designed, edited and
project-managed
for DK by Dynamo Ltd.**

First published in Great Britain in 2017 by
Dorling Kindersley Limited
80 Strand, London, WC2R 0RL

A CIP catalogue record for this book
is available from the British Library.
ISBN: 978-0-2413-3661-8

Printed and bound in Romania

A WORLD OF IDEAS:
SEE ALL THERE IS TO KNOW

www.dk.com

Acknowledgements:
The publisher would like to thank the following people
for their help in photographing, designing, making, and
handling slime: Tony Limerick, Tim Pestridge, Elissa
Rowson, Olivia Chin-Yue, Mia Pestridge, Leo Sandford,
and Bridget Stanley. Special thanks to Evie Allan
for inspiring us to create this book.

Contents

Non-edible Slime

🍴 Edible Slime

Basic Slime Kit

These are the essentials needed for most of the recipes in this book...

bowls

measuring spoons

mixing spoon or spatula

clear craft glue   PVA glue

cornflour   eyewash   bicarbonate of soda   shaving foam

Here are some of the extras you'll need. Check each recipe for specific ingredients.

finger and poster paint

plastic beads, gems and pompoms

glitter glue

food colouring   glitter   googly eyes

Most ingredients in this book are easy to find, but if you can't get certain items, ask an adult to buy them or order them online.

Non-edible Slime

Yuk! Don't be tempted to eat these. We love making a slime mess, but make sure you clear up anything you may spill or drop. Ready? The slime fun is just over the page...

Basic Slime

TIME:
5 MINUTES

DIFFICULTY:
EASY

WARNING:
NON-EDIBLE

This is the easiest recipe, but one of the most amazing. Watch as your slime turns from a solid to a liquid and back again in seconds!

YOU WILL NEED

* cornflour
* water
* food colouring

1

Scoop a few big spoonfuls of cornflour into a bowl.

2

Add drops of water bit by bit until you have a thick slime.

3

Grab a handful of slime and squelch together. Keep your hands moving to keep the mixture solid. When you stop, the slime will change back into a liquid.

Stir in a few drops
of food colouring
for a blast of colour.

⚠️ **MAY STAIN!**

SCIENCE BIT

If you try to hit this slime, it will act like a solid and you'll get sore knuckles. If you gently poke your finger inside the mixture, it will feel like a liquid. Strange, huh? Hundreds of years ago famous scientist Sir Isaac Newton wrote about how liquids behave. Slime like this is known as a non-Newtonian fluid because it doesn't play by his rules!

Stretchy Slime

TIME:
10 MINUTES

DIFFICULTY:
EASY

WARNING:
NON-EDIBLE

This is a super-fun recipe to try. This gloopy stuff is the basis for many more awesome slimes later in the book.

YOU WILL NEED

* 240 ml (8 ½ fl oz) PVA glue
* 1 tsp bicarbonate of soda
* finger paint or food colouring of your choice
* 1 tbs eyewash – it must contain boric acid and sodium borate

1

Pour the glue and bicarbonate of soda into your bowl. Beat together.

2

Squirt in some paint and stir well. Keep adding more paint until you get the perfect colour.

3

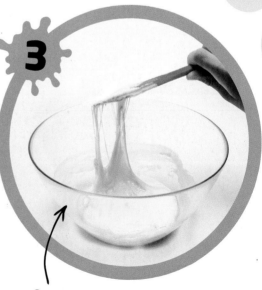

Drop in the eyewash and mix together. The slime will begin to get stringy. When it comes away from the edges of the bowl, knead or squish the mixture with your hands.

SCIENCE BIT

Glue is made of long molecules (groups of atoms) called polymers. When glue and eyewash are mixed, the polymers stick together. This turns glue from a liquid into a bouncy, stretchy solid.

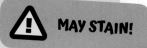

MAY STAIN!

9

Fluffy Slime

TIME:
10 MINUTES

DIFFICULTY:
EASY

WARNING:
NON-EDIBLE

Beat up a storm with this super-soft, foamy recipe. It might feel like clouds of marshmallow, but this slime is NOT to eat!

YOU WILL NEED

* 480 ml (17 fl oz) shaving foam (not gel)
* food colouring of your choice
* 60 ml (2 fl oz) PVA glue
* ¼ tsp bicarbonate of soda
* 1 tbs eyewash – it must contain boric acid and sodium borate

1

Mix together the shaving foam and a few drops of food colouring. Then stir in the glue and the bicarbonate of soda. Make sure it's all fully blended.

2

Whip in the eyewash. When the mixture starts to get stringy, you're almost there.

3

Hands at the ready! Knead the slime until puffy and soft. Add more eyewash if your mixture is too sticky.

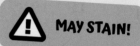

MAY STAIN!

See-through Slime

Good slime comes to those who wait. Hang on in there for a week as the bubbles slowly burst. Then it will be clear to see why this is also known as glass slime.

YOU WILL NEED

* ½ tsp bicarbonate of soda
* 120 ml (4 fl oz) warm water
* 140 ml (5 fl oz) clear craft glue
* eyewash – it must contain boric acid and sodium borate

SCIENCE BIT

Some animals make slime, too. Hagfish create a thick, gloopy, see-through ooze to put attackers off. For this reason they are sometimes known as snot eels!

1

Put the bicarbonate of soda and water into your bowl.

2

Mix in the clear glue. Then stir in small amounts of eyewash until the mixture starts to gloop together.

TIME:
5 - 7 DAYS

DIFFICULTY:
EASY

WARNING:
NON-EDIBLE

3

Keep mixing until your slime forms a big, see-through ball with bubbles inside. Check your slime every day until the bubbles have disappeared, and then play!

13

Serious Putty

TIME:
15 MINUTES

DIFFICULTY:
EASY

WARNING:
NON-EDIBLE

Have fun making this simple two-ingredient recipe. Once you've made this super soft and stretchy slime, you won't be able to stop playing with it!

YOU WILL NEED

* reusable sticky tack
* liquid hand soap

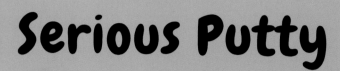

1

Take a strip of sticky tack. Stretch the tack and play with it until it softens.

2

Pour some liquid soap into a small bowl. Dip the tack into the liquid soap and squish it together.

3

Continue to dip the tack into the liquid soap and work together. You will find the tack becomes more stretchy as you go. Don't add too much soap or the putty will become sticky.

15

Starry Slime

A sprinkle of neon sparkle will give this slime an out-of-this world shine.

TIME:
10 MINUTES

DIFFICULTY:
EASY

WARNING:
NON-EDIBLE

YOU WILL NEED

* ½ tsp bicarbonate of soda
* 120 ml (4 fl oz) warm water
* 140 ml (5 fl oz) clear craft glue
* neon purple glitter
* eyewash – it must contain boric acid and sodium borate
* star confetti
* star glitter

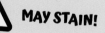 **MAY STAIN!**

How about...?

This is a great slime to make at a birthday party. Instead of star confetti, grab bags of number confetti – for how old you're going to be!

1

Mix together the bicarbonate of soda, water, and clear glue. Pour neon glitter on top. You shouldn't need food colouring. The glitter should be enough to add colour and sparkle.

2

Stir in small splashes of eyewash until the slime doesn't stick to your fingers.

3

Add star confetti and more glitter. To give your slime real depth, try to find stars of different sizes. Mix everything together with your hands, and play!

Crunchy Slime

TIME:
10 MINUTES

DIFFICULTY:
EASY

WARNING:
NON-EDIBLE

Use this recipe to make some seriously gruesome goo with added crunch! Why not make this slime at Halloween?

YOU WILL NEED

* ½ tsp bicarbonate of soda
* 120 ml (4 fl oz) warm water
* 140 ml (5 fl oz) clear craft glue
* red food colouring
* eyewash – it must contain boric acid and sodium borate
* plastic beads

1

Mix bicarbonate of soda, water, and clear glue. Add a few drops of red food colouring and stir.

2

Drop in a little eyewash at a time. Beat the mixture together until it stops sticking to the bowl.

3

Add a handful or two of plastic beads. Fold them into the slime using your hands. Let the gory fun begin!

TOP TIP!

The beads will make a crunching noise as they grind against each other. See how many you can put into your slime mix and find out how the sound changes.

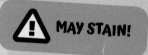 MAY STAIN!

Smelly Slime

Slime looks good and feels good, so now it's time to find out how to make it smell good, too!

YOU WILL NEED

* 240 ml (8½ fl oz) PVA glue
* 1 tsp bicarbonate of soda
* red and yellow finger paint
* a few drops of your choice of food flavouring
* 1 tbs eyewash – it must contain boric acid and sodium borate

TIME:
5 MINUTES

DIFFICULTY:
EASY

WARNING:
NON-EDIBLE

MAY STAIN!

TOP TIP!

As yummy as this slime smells, don't be tempted to take a quick bite! Why not make a trick slime that doesn't smell so nice? Try combining food flavouring that shouldn't go together!

1

Mix the glue and bicarbonate of soda into your bowl. Squirt in the paint and stir well. Experiment by mixing different paint colours together to get your perfect orange shade.

2

Now it's time to make your slime smell like an orange, too. Splash in some flavouring and stir.

3

Next add the eyewash. The slime will start to come away from the sides of the bowl. Knead the mixture with your hands until it stops sticking to your fingers.

Glitter Slime

You can add glitter to lots of slime recipes, but it sparkles best when added to see-through slime.

YOU WILL NEED

* 45 ml (3 packets of) peel-off face masks – they must contain polyvinyl alcohol
* glitter
* 1 tsp bicarbonate of soda
* eyewash – it must contain boric acid and sodium borate

TIME:
5 MINUTES

DIFFICULTY:
EASY

WARNING:
NON-EDIBLE

⚠ **MAY STAIN!**

1

After emptying the face masks into a bowl, sprinkle in some glitter. Try adding different colours and sizes of glitter for extra sparkle.

2

Stir in the bicarbonate of soda.

3

Glitter works really well
in see-through slime
(see pages 12-13).

Add splashes of eyewash and mix
until the slime starts to come together.
Slime-making can take a bit of trial
and error, so use your judgement.

Popping Slime

Want to make your slime go POP? This noisy slime looks like something spooky left behind by a ghost – oooohhhh!

YOU WILL NEED

* ½ tsp bicarbonate of soda
* 120 ml (4 fl oz) warm water
* 140 ml (5 fl oz) clear craft glue
* a couple of drops of green food colouring
* eyewash – it must contain boric acid and sodium borate
* popping candy

1

Put two or three drops of green food colouring into a mixture of bicarbonate of soda, water, and glue.

2

Add eyewash bit by bit until your slime goes stringy and starts to come away from the sides of the bowl.

3

Sprinkle in as much popping candy as you want. Then stick your hands in the bowl and mix everything together. Your slime will start popping as you play with it.

TIME:
10 MINUTES

DIFFICULTY:
EASY

WARNING:
NON-EDIBLE

POP!

POP!

POP!

POP!

POP!

POP!

POP!

SCIENCE BIT

The noise popping candy makes is caused by tiny bubbles of carbon dioxide bursting out of it. The gas is trapped in very hot, melted sugar under very high pressure. When the popping candy cools and hardens, the carbon dioxide can't escape until it gets wet.

Slimy Shades of Colour

One of the best things about slime is you choose how it looks. Experiment with different colours and shades of paint. Layer and twist your slime to form your very own eye-catching creation!

YOU WILL NEED

FOR EACH SLIME SHADE:

* about 120 ml (4 fl oz) PVA glue
* ½ tsp bicarbonate of soda
* finger paint
* ½ tbs eyewash – it must contain boric acid and sodium borate

⚠ **MAY STAIN!**

1

Put 120 ml glue and ½ tsp bicarbonate of soda into each of your four bowls. Add different amounts of the same colour paint to three of the batches.

Leave your first batch paint-free!

Add ½ tsp of paint to your second batch.

Add 1 tsp of paint to your third batch.

Lastly, add 2 tbs of paint to your fourth batch!

2

After you have stirred in the paint, add in ½ tbs of eyewash to each bowl to make the slime form.

3

Layer up your colours or shades and twist them around.

TOP TIP!
. . . .
Any slime with stripes won't stay stripy for long. The more you play with your slime, the more the colours will blend together.

Gold Slime

If you're not careful, your gold slime might end up a nasty brown mess! Add some sparkly jewels to give your slime extra bling.

⚠ **MAY STAIN!**

YOU WILL NEED

* ½ tsp bicarbonate of soda
* 120 ml (4 fl oz) warm water
* 140 ml (5 fl oz) clear craft glue
* gold poster paint
* eyewash – it must contain boric acid and sodium borate
* plastic jewels or beads

1

Mix together the bicarbonate of soda, water, and glue. Squirt in gold paint and stir until you're happy with the shade.

2

Add the eyewash
bit by bit and stir until
the slime comes together.

3

Sprinkle the plastic jewels or beads
on the top of the mixture and fold
them in using your hands. Now play!

If you can't get
hold of gold paint,
why not try some
gold glitter to
really make your
slime shine?

TOP TIP!

Use clear glue to get the
best result when mixing
with gold paint. Don't
forget to wash your
hands when finished!

Unicorn Slime

This super-fluffy unicorn slime is the biggest challenge yet. It makes more slime than any other recipe in this book!

YOU WILL NEED

FOR EACH SLIME COLOUR:

* 480 ml (17 fl oz) shaving foam (not gel)
* food colouring (try yellow, blue, green, and red)
* 60 ml (2 fl oz) PVA glue
* ¼ tsp bicarbonate of soda
* 1 tbs eyewash – it must contain boric acid and sodium borate
* glitter

1

Make four batches of Fluffy Slime (see pages 10-11 for the method). Use a different food colouring for each mixture.

TIME:
40 MINUTES

DIFFICULTY:
HARD

WARNING:
NON-EDIBLE

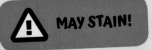

⚠ **MAY STAIN!**

2

Sprinkle plenty of glitter into each bowl. Now stir.

3

Lay your slimes out in strips and get your hands in there!

Metallic Slime

TIME:
10 MINUTES

DIFFICULTY:
EASY

WARNING:
NON-EDIBLE

Seek out special ingredients like lustre dust to give your slime a real shine!

YOU WILL NEED

* ½ tsp bicarbonate of soda
* 120 ml (4 fl oz) warm water
* 140 ml (5 fl oz) clear craft glue
* lustre dust
* eyewash – it must contain boric acid and sodium borate

1

Mix together the bicarbonate of soda, water, and clear glue. Sprinkle plenty of lustre dust on top.

2

You won't need any additional colour for this slime – the dust should be all you need. Stir it in.

3

Add drops of eyewash a little at a time. As you stir, your mixture will start to gloop together. When it comes away from the sides of the bowl, your slime is ready for some serious stretching!

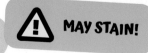

⚠ MAY STAIN!

33

Sand Slime

TIME:
10 MINUTES

DIFFICULTY:
EASY

WARNING:
NON-EDIBLE

There are loads of ways to add texture to your slime. Here is one of the simplest.

YOU WILL NEED

* ½ tsp bicarbonate of soda
* 120 ml (4 fl oz) warm water
* 140 ml (5 fl oz) clear craft glue
* yellow food colouring
* eyewash – it must contain boric acid and sodium borate
* play sand

SCIENCE BIT

Sand is made when rocks are broken down into small grains. It comes in lots of different colours and textures. Did you know that the colour of sand varies because of the kind of rock that it comes from?

1

Mix together the bicarbonate of soda, water, glue, and a few drops of food colouring.

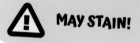 **MAY STAIN!**

2

Add drops of eyewash to turn your mixture into slime. You will know it's ready when the slime doesn't stick to the sides of the bowl anymore.

3

Fold in some play sand with your hands. Add more until it feels gritty.

Monster Slime

Add googly eyes for awesome slime that looks like a melted monster!

YOU WILL NEED

* about 120 ml (4 fl oz) PVA glue
* ½ tsp bicarbonate of soda
* green finger paint, or a mix of blue and yellow finger paints
* ½ tbs eyewash – it must contain boric acid and sodium borate
* googly eyes

TIME: **5 MINUTES**

DIFFICULTY: **EASY**

WARNING: **NON-EDIBLE**

Mix the glue and bicarbonate of soda. Squirt in blue and yellow paint. Keep mixing. Getting the right shade of green will be a bit of an experiment in colour. Or if you have it, just use green paint!

Beat in the eyewash. You'll know when the slime is coming together when it turns stringy.

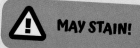

3

TOP TIP!
. . . .

Try other paint colours, or mix two colours together, for a swirly, melted mess of a monster!

When the slime doesn't stick to the bowl anymore, it's ready. Make a splat of slime on a plastic mat and add googly eyes to create your melted monster!

Snow Slime

YOU WILL NEED

* 360-480 ml (12½-17 fl oz) shaving foam (not gel)
* 60 ml (2 fl oz) PVA glue
* ¼ tsp bicarbonate of soda
* 1 tbs eyewash – it must contain boric acid and sodium borate
* small polystyrene balls

TIME:
15 MINUTES

DIFFICULTY:
EASY

WARNING:
NON-EDIBLE

1

Make half a batch of Fluffy Slime (see pages 10-11), but without food colouring.

Gradually fold in the polystyrene balls. The slime should hold them in place nicely. You can add as many balls as you like.

2

⚠️ **MAY STAIN!**

Add paint to this recipe to get a great textured and colourful slime you'll love to squish!

TOP TIP!
. . . .

Don't play with slime in a room with carpets! Stick to playing on hard floors, or even better, go outside. If you drop any blobs, white vinegar should dissolve any dried-in slime accidents.

Fake Snot

TIME:
2 HOURS

DIFFICULTY:
INTERMEDIATE

WARNING:
NON-EDIBLE

Time for a super-slimy, revolting recipe. It's perfect for Halloween or to gross-out your family and friends! Just make sure a grown-up helps you with the boiling water.

YOU WILL NEED

* 120 ml (4 fl oz) boiling water
* 3 tsp gelatin
* 60 ml (2 fl oz) golden syrup
* green food colouring

SCIENCE BIT

Snot may not look pretty, but it's super-useful. It stops germs and dust from being sucked up our noses and down into our lungs.

Ask a grown-up to carefully pour hot water into the small bowl and sprinkle the gelatin on top. Stir together with a fork.

1

⚠ **BOILING WATER!**

2

Next, add the food colouring. Drop in a splash at a time until you get a snotty shade of green. Don't touch the mixture until it has cooled for about an hour.

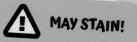
MAY STAIN!

3

The green mixture will start to form a jelly. Slowly add it to a bowl with the golden syrup in. The slime should create strings of snot-like substance. Yuk!

Pompom Slime

TIME:
10 MINUTES

DIFFICULTY:
EASY

WARNING:
NON-EDIBLE

See-through slime looks even better when you accessorize it! Try out this cool way of adding colour and texture.

YOU WILL NEED

* ½ tsp bicarbonate of soda
* 120 ml (4 fl oz) warm water
* 140 ml (5 fl oz) clear craft glue
* eyewash – it must contain boric acid and sodium borate
* packet of mini pompoms

1

Make up a batch of See-through Slime (see pages 12-13). You don't need to wait a week to use this mixture though. The bubbles add to the look!

2

Empty a packet of pompoms into the slime. Fold them in using your hands.

3

See how far your polka-dot slime can stretch!

How about...?

Add plastic alphabet tiles to your slime rather than pompoms. Then squish the slime about to make words or your name. Don't add too many pieces though – they'll fall out!

Winter Wonderland Slime

This is a simple and quick way to theme your slime. Vary it with different wintry colours and confetti. Unleash your imagination!

Try this one after mastering See-through Slime (see pages 12-13). This version uses part clear glue and part glitter glue, but the recipe is just the same, and you don't need to wait for the bubbles to clear.

YOU WILL NEED

* ½ tsp bicarbonate of soda
* 120 ml (4 fl oz) warm water
* 140 ml (5 fl oz) mixture of clear craft glue and light-blue glitter glue
* eyewash – it must contain boric acid and sodium borate
* snowflake confetti
* extra glitter (optional)

TIME:
10 MINUTES

DIFFICULTY:
EASY

WARNING:
NON-EDIBLE

Fold in the snowflake confetti. The great thing about slime is there is no right or wrong when it comes to adding extras. You can put in as much or as little confetti as you like.

2

3

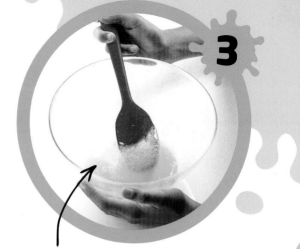

If you don't think your slime has enough sparkle, fold in a big sprinkle of glitter.

SCIENCE BIT

This type of snowflake is also known as a snow crystal. No two snow crystals look the same. This is because their patterns depend on how they fall through clouds.

Dinosaurs in Amber

Discover dinosaur treasures hidden deep inside this prehistoric slime!

YOU WILL NEED

* ½ tsp bicarbonate of soda
* 120 ml (4 fl oz) warm water
* 140 ml (5 fl oz) clear craft glue
* yellow food colouring
* yellow glitter
* gold lustre dust
* eyewash – it must contain boric acid and sodium borate
* small plastic dinosaur toys

1

Add food colouring, glitter, and lustre dust to a mixture of bicarbonate of soda, water, and glue. Make sure you don't add too much food colouring – the colour shouldn't be overpowering.

2

Beat in the eyewash until the amber mixture becomes stringy and comes away from the bowl.

3

Drop in plastic dinosaur toys and see if your the slime is sticky enough for them not to fall out.

TIME:
10 MINUTES

DIFFICULTY:
EASY

WARNING:
NON-EDIBLE

SCIENCE BIT

Amber is a liquid that oozes from prehistoric trees and then becomes as hard as rock over time. Ancient insect and dinosaur parts have been found trapped inside lumps of amber!

⚠ MAY STAIN!

Bubbling Swamp Slime

Mixing bicarbonate of soda and vinegar makes this slime bubble – this is called a chemical reaction. The result is a slime that belongs on an alien planet!

1

YOU WILL NEED

* 480 ml (17 fl oz) white vinegar
* 1¼ tsp xanthan gum
* green food colouring or a mix of other colours to make a murky green colour
* bicarbonate of soda

Put the vinegar, xanthan gum, and drops of food colouring in a bowl. Stir it all together. Don't worry if your mixture is a little lumpy – that's exactly what you want!

SCIENCE BIT

This slime is bubbly because of the way vinegar and bicarbonate of soda react to each other. They produce carbon dioxide. You could also use lemon juice instead of vinegar as it is an acid, too!

2

Once you've finished stirring your mixture, put it in the fridge for a few hours until it has thickened.

3

Place a thick layer of bicarbonate of soda in the bottom of a clean bowl. Then cover it with the green gloop. Bubbles will pop up through the mix and glug away for some time.

⚠️ MAY STAIN!

Bubble Slime

Slime is not just for stretching and squidging ...
why not try blowing bubbles with it?

YOU WILL NEED

* about 240 ml (8½ fl oz) PVA glue
* 1 tsp bicarbonate of soda
* pink food colouring
* 1 tbs eyewash – it must contain boric acid and sodium borate

1

Make up a batch of Stretchy Slime (see pages 8-9), but this time use pink food colouring.

2

Stick a straw in the slime. Pinch around the edges at the bottom to make sure the straw is air-tight. This means no air can escape through the hole.

3

Blow slowly and steadily to make the biggest bubble you can! When it pops, reposition your straw and blow another one.

TIME:
10 MINUTES

DIFFICULTY:
INTERMEDIATE

WARNING:
NON-EDIBLE

SAFETY FIRST!

This slime is thick and unlikely to go up
your straw. But make sure you don't suck –
nobody wants a mouthful of slime. Gross!

DO NOT
INHALE!

51

Glow-in-the-Dark

This recipe is so simple but has amazing results.
Switch off the lights and get the glow going!

YOU WILL NEED

* ½ tsp bicarbonate of soda
* 120 ml (4 fl oz) warm water
* 140 ml (5 fl oz) clear craft glue
* glow-in-the-dark poster paint
* eyewash – it must contain boric acid and sodium borate

1

Squirt plenty of glow-in-the-dark poster paint into a bowl containing bicarbonate of soda, water, and glue.

2

Stir in the paint and add eyewash, bit by bit. When the slime stops sticking to the bowl, it's almost ready.

3

Switch off the light and mix your slime with your hands. This slime works best when it's still gloopy. Don't forget to wash your hands when you've finished playing!

TIME:
10 MINUTES

DIFFICULTY:
EASY

WARNING:
NON-EDIBLE

TOP TIP!

You'll need to charge up your slime so you can see it in the dark. Shine a torch on it to get it glowing brightly!

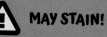 **MAY STAIN!**

Edible Slime

Make sure you have plenty of cornflour to stop these slimes sticking to surfaces, and to you! Grab an adult when making these recipes – hot equipment is needed. Always check with a grown-up before handling slimes that have been heated and don't eat all at once!

Chocolate Goo

Perfect for playing a trick on someone,
this slime looks yucky, but tastes yummy!

YOU WILL NEED

* ½ 397g-tin condensed milk
* 2 tbs chocolate sauce
* 1 tbs cornflour

TIME:
1 HOUR

DIFFICULTY:
HARD

WARNING:
EDIBLE SLIME

1

Empty half a tin of condensed
milk into a saucepan. Add the
chocolate sauce and stir in well.

2

Mix in the cornflour and ask an adult to put the saucepan on a low heat. Stir until the mixture thickens. Transfer the slime into a bowl and leave to cool. A grown-up will be able to tell you when it's safe to touch.

⚠️ **HOT!**

3

How about...?

Try adding some tasty, crunchy snacks to the slime. Chocolate chips will go down a treat and make it even more chocolatey! Or maybe raisins or dried fruit? Add a handful in Step 3 when the slime has cooled down enough to be squished.

Sieve cornflour over your slime. Sprinkle some onto your hands, too. This will stop it sticking to you quite so much. Then get in there and squish that slime!

57

Sticky, Icky, Tasty Slime

Some of the recipes in this book look good enough to eat, but you definitely shouldn't eat them. However, this one is completely edible. Yum!

YOU WILL NEED

* packet of marshmallows – we used 10 big marshmallows, but you can try this with as many or as few as you like

* a couple of spoonfuls of cornflour

* a couple of spoonfuls of icing sugar

⚠ **HOT!**

⚠ **HOT!**

Sieve over equal amounts of cornflour and icing sugar. Add them a little at a time – not too much or your slime will be too tough to handle and might not taste as good. Stir together using a spoon. No touching! It's still hot.

Place your marshmallows in a bowl and ask an adult to microwave on full power for 10 seconds. Repeat until melted. Don't touch yet as it'll be mega hot! Wait a few minutes for the mixture to cool.

3

TOP TIP!

This is much stickier than most slime recipes. The best thing is, you can lick your hands clean when you've finished playing with this one! Just remember to wash your hands before making and handling this slime. And always clean up after yourself!

Get a grown-up to test the temperature of the slime. If it's nice and cool, stick your hands in and enjoy. Don't eat it all at once!

The Bear Necessities

Melting sweets makes a slime that smells and tastes delicious. Melted gummy bears end up more like a putty than a slime!

YOU WILL NEED

* a few packs of gummy bears
* cornflour
* icing sugar

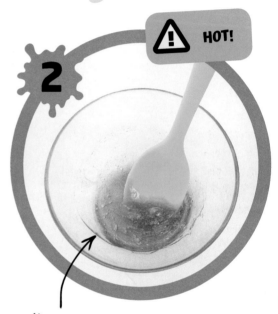

⚠ HOT!

You will have a lovely, glassy, melted mixture, but watch out – it will be super-hot! Stir it carefully with a spoon, or ask a grown up to help.

⚠ HOT!

Pick out all of the bears of your favourite colour. Put them in a bowl and ask an adult to microwave on full power for 10 seconds. Repeat until they've all melted.

TOP TIP!

The amount of cornflour and icing sugar needed depends on how many gummy bears you use. Start off with little spoonfuls and increase until you've got it just right. The cornflour stops the slime sticking to you, but the icing sugar keeps it tasting sweet!

3

TIME:
15 MINUTES

DIFFICULTY:
INTERMEDIATE

WARNING:
EDIBLE SLIME

Add equal amounts of cornflour and icing sugar and stir. Let it cool. Ask a grown-up to test the temperature. When it's cool enough to handle, scoop it all up and have lots of fun!

Stripy Slime

YOU WILL NEED

* several packets of chewy sweets – make sure you have four different colours!
* icing sugar
* cornflour

TIME:
30 MINUTES

DIFFICULTY:
HARD

WARNING:
EDIBLE SLIME

1

⚠ **HOT!**

Unwrap your chewy sweets and put each colour into a different bowl. Ask an adult to microwave each bowl of sweets on full power for 10 seconds. Repeat until all of the sweets have melted.

2

Sieve a mixture of icing sugar and cornflour onto a clean surface. Spoon out each bowl of melted chewy sweets onto the dusted surface to cool. Ask a grown-up to let you know when the blobs are cool enough to handle.

3

Sieve more icing sugar and cornflour on top of each blob. Roll each colour into a long sausage shape. Layer the colours and twist them about. When you've had enough, just take a bite!

TOP TIP!
. . . .

Make sure you have plenty of cornflour to stop this slime sticking to surfaces, and to you! The more you stretch it, the less sticky it should become.

Slime Storage

You need to look after your slime carefully to stop it drying out. Make sure you have airtight containers to store your creations and keep them clean and slime-y.

plastic boxes with lids   zip-lock bags

Cleaning Up

You won't be popular if you make a mess, so follow these rules...

* Always make slime on a wipe-clean surface.
* There's always a risk of staining with paint or food colouring, so lay down some paper first.
* Mop up and wash up any soon as you can.
* Wash hands before and after handling slime.
* Wipe down all surfaces and put your slime kit and ingredients away.
* NEVER pour slime failures down the sink – you'll block the drains!
* Always ask an adult before using cleaning products or washing up.

Hints and Tips

The recipes in this book should be easy to make, but slightly different ingredients may change the texture of the slime. With a bit of trial and error you should be able to get the results you want, but here are a few pointers.

MY GLUE-BASED SLIME IS TOO STICKY!
Add a few more drops of eyewash and mix in well. Keep adding until the right consistency.

MY EDIBLE SLIME IS TOO STICKY!
Cover your hands with cornflour or add more into the mix , but remember the mess is part of the fun!

MY SLIME BREAKS WHEN I STRETCH IT!
Sounds like you've added too much eyewash. Try squirting a small amount of the glue you've used onto your slime and carefully fold it in.

MY SLIME ISN'T GLITTERY ENOUGH!
If you're using PVA glue make sure you've got a chunky glitter rather than a fine one otherwise it will get lost. And remember the key rule when making a glittery slime – add some glitter, then add some more!

MY SLIME IS GOING HARD!
Slime doesn't last forever! Perhaps it's time to make your next batch? What will you make this time?